Capillarity

ARTO VAUN was born in Cambridge, MA and has attended the University of Massachusetts Boston, Bennington College, and Harvard University. He has taught at Glasgow University and the University of Massachusetts, Boston. He was co-founder and co-editor of the literary journal *Aspora* while living in Los Angeles, was co-editor of *The Armenian Weekly* in Boston, and a correspondent to *AIM Magazine*. He is also a songwriter and musician, releasing albums as Mishima USA and The Kent 100s. In other lives he has worked as an ESL instructor, journalist, cutlery salesman, jeweller's apprentice, and a teacher's aide at Hollywood public schools. He is studying for a PhD in English Literature/Creative Writing at Glasgow University and lives somewhere in the middle of the Atlantic, between Scotland and Boston.

T0148800

CARCANET

ARTO VAUN

Capillarity

CARCANET

First published in Great Britain in 2009 by
Carcanet Press Limited
Alliance House
Cross Street
Manchester M2 7AQ

A CIP catalogue record for this book is available from the British Library
ISBN 978 1 85754 991 1

The publisher acknowledges financial assistance from Arts Council England

Typeset by XL Publishing Services, Tiverton
Printed and bound in England by SRP Ltd, Exeter

In memory of my father

I am not to speak to you—I am to think of you when I sit alone, or wake a night alone,
I am to wait—I do not doubt I am to meet you again,
I am to see to it that I do not lose you.

Walt Whitman

cap·il·lar·i·ty

n. The interaction between contacting surfaces of a liquid and a solid that distorts the liquid surface.

I

America, now I will try it this way:
All my years, after all, are bursting yellow-blue on this day
And I am walking as we all have walked on pavement and roads
Treading on each other's struggling skin-souls
      Trampling without knowing any better

Our towns are forgetful and we are only human though we have built
And burned down—we toss and turn in our sleep and wake up grumpy

So let them come forward, who cannot see straight
Let them come forward, who are on fire, all crackling heat
Let them come forward, whose weak knees are those of a wounded elk
Let them come forward, who have been nudged off the map
Let them come forward, who have forgiven and cry while driving
Let them come forward, who smell the cut grass and the wound around the corner
Let them come forward, who are my kin, your kin, and there when our hands sweat

Is it possibly in the way the finch flew close to my sun-veiled face
      When I was so close to home—
It took something with it from me as I felt the weight of its wings
Maybe something I wanted taken

Forget everything you know, I told myself, because you have started
To see glimpses of what it is really that inches toward you
Like a cluster of sparkling universes in a baby's palm
      That you take to your lips

I was so close

II

Your father, tender mechanic under the Olds on freezing ground
In 1987—you can hear the work going on and wonder about his back
And hands in the snowy dark beneath the car's belly as he asks you
      To hold the flashlight steady—hold it steady
Upon the engine he will fix so we can get from here to there

      Then, I was not my father as you are not yours
But let's be clear—we are illuminated residue, threaded—
Check underneath your fingernails

      I tried to hold the light steady

III

Who will put out their hand
So that we can be pulled along when we are tired—

There is a reckoning, so they say,
But I am not convinced since everywhere the living are spiteful toward the dead

Whose silvery litter is molecular
Whose names are scrambled codes beyond spelling
Whose love and hate hug the hug of reconciled siblings
Whose stillness is the stillness of a mute river in winter
Whose bones whimper and gossip only in our telling
Whose judgment is in the mirror as we walk by

    They are industrious as pasts

IV

One day I woke up unlike other wakings
And saw my hands for the first time as though they had sprouted
Overnight, while I was missing you again—my open palm and branched fingers
In the smudged morning light

I looked at what seemed a memory or shy wolf
That toils without asking for much except to eat and be taken seriously—
      My hands were severe then

What is the elastic that tightens in the body when you forget to let go
      Or be let go of—

V

In 1920, playing under a tree, my grandfather is clueless
About the hill he will stand on one black winter night twenty-nine years later
As he tries to go to work at the sewing factory—he sees radiant eyes hovering below
That shine with an intention he does not recognize
They seem to know him somehow

He decides, pulls his wool coat taut around himself, sits on the snow
And slides down the hill—the man at the bottom was scared of the eyes
He saw at the top gazing down at him—
They both light a cigarette after moving on, trembling to themselves
Each relieved the other was not a wolf

Now, sometimes when I walk into the future I think about how gone he is—
How gone, my father, grandfather, uncle, aunt, friends, lovers—

Perhaps I recognize my dead and wounded in strangers who wait for the bus with me
Perhaps I feel them in my sleep, dark-winged and sour
Perhaps they gaze at me when I am shaming myself
Or perhaps they could care less and are rumors I am hoarding

Who will answer for the chatter and stares that outline our paths
Who will speak in tongues to rattle the coma in this land

VI

Mother, you are pale as water and have the intentions of a tulip
      Caught in wind

Sometimes in my dreams I am yelling at you

            I am sorry, as I think you are

But an ache is hard to figure
      There have always been thistles and drought between us
We have been stupidly parched from history I guess

      One day, I am twelve years old, playing the piano (as I have taught myself)
I like the black keys, the incongruity gives a comfort lacking in people
You are all sitting in the living room as I make up pretty good songs, for a kid

      No one has died yet, so we are as dumb as ever about what hangs
      Above our heads

You are always the first to shut me down
Stop that noise we're trying to talk

      Then the others start, repeating, except dad and grandma
The cracks inside me render everything gigantic outside my puny self—
      That you did not mean it means little now

      A boy sitting on a piano bench, hands still

VII

My kin, I decided to listen to you, to look at what happened to you
To make you coiled in yourselves, restless mutes and ambitious cripples
To make you pick away at your futures until there were scabs everywhere
To make you hold your kids almost in contempt for being open as oceans
To make you slap with one hand and embrace with the other everything about you
        Until your children were the ones bruising, dizzy

For a long time when I saw myself all I could recognize was humiliation and
        Insignificance
So well bred that many years were spent harassing and exiling myself, finding
Enormous airtight defeats everywhere, mapping them out in my head
        No compass, no key

Cartography is not a precise science no matter what satellites say—
Territories shift the way a wife and husband notice one day that they have
Forgotten to spare each other

That is how the land under our feet is, and our soaked hearts

VIII

Forgotten the late night hand of an ex-girlfriend in 1994, dragging me out of bed
Because the Los Angeles floor was shaking—boisterous drunk timpani players
Improvising for the traces of sweethearts
   Who are only annoyed now

I tell you this
     No one is safe anyway and everyway
   Yet so beautiful the standing around in the heat while a whole county squirms
And says
     I am fucking right here! while you are in your pajama bottoms
     Paper stars that want to be the real thing so bad, but can only
Go back to bed, sorry cases all
        Nothing they can do

Up in the trees and A/C ducts and television towers the dead blush for us
   See, how shy

Sweetheart, they were the ones that told me to leave you that night
How it broke me more than the earth broke parts of the freeway
   But I was twenty-three and decidedly choking on my father's dust
Fixed in a canyon beyond your selfless reach

     Thinking of that terrain still horrifies me because I know
My father wanders there, on the moon-glazed canyon floor
In his beige-collared shirt, short-sleeves rolled up a bit, chewing Wrigley's mint gum
    Trying to reach a plateau every night,
Every night his black leather shoes getting so dirty

All he wants is to find his wife and son
He does not know how he suddenly woke up there
And does not get used to it no matter what

Poor, poor dad, you are dead
   And your son sits here wanting nothing more
   Than to be as impoverished as you,
If only to smell the Old Spice and cigarettes on your suit jacket and make you hurt—
     The tightest hug that canyon has ever known

That is how we think about our dead when we do not want to die
Do not want to talk about it really, the way we don't like to talk
About falling out of love

                    I could not tell you that then, standing in your driveway—
Forgiving myself has taken this long

And still an empire sits its fat ass on my chest

IX

So many mistakes I've made so rightly—
Water travels the only way it knows

I became a string quartet, a minimalist one
It happened somewhere on the 10 in New Mexico, on my way
Back to Boston, the car without heat

I admit, it was not spelled out for me at the time
I was just cold and tired from days of driving alone
My father's little boy, my mother's only son
A fugitive moved to tears by distant random homes
Isolated toys in the wide distance, landscapes
Trekked by families a century ago, looking for mercy—

It must have been so, so quiet then—
Just ill-fitting shoes making that addictive crunch on the earth

Crunch crunch
And what must have been a terrible endless horizon

Crunch crunch

Only when they had to bury children was it worse

X

Somewhere in my grandmother's apartment there is a photograph:
Two infant boys, around 1945 or so, although it looks more like 1920

They are looking at the camera the way children used to—
Already sullen adult gazes, dressed in white frilly gowns

My two uncles—they sit together with an understanding
That they shall not inherit the earth, but die in a few weeks

From malnutrition and insufficient medical care—look closer
And you can see they are fading right in your hand

My grandparents, resilient granite angels, could not talk
About this one thing—they themselves were children

When they buried their own, left them in a small Armenian cemetery
Leaving one land not theirs to another not theirs to another not theirs

America, your homeless are not the beggars and street people—
They are the hop-scotching peasants whose nations are anxious myths now

The crowd asks
What did you expect going out alone like that—

History wears pantyhose over its head and gets away with murder every time

XI

They had a destination—
It was of dried molasses and bitter root and thimbles
It was in the one pair of shoes each could afford

More than once my mother or her sisters fell in the snow
On the way to school, on the way home
And lost a shoe
                The roads were not paved then in Yerevan
They would cry like the women they would become thousands of miles later

          One little naked foot

Grandmother was a girl herself
But in the cold slit of dawn she would go
Stand in line for clothes, bread, some meat

         A line
            Of mostly young women
                    In 1949, their legs freezing

Some of them wished they were dead

After hours of standing, sometimes nothing to bring home

XII

The road from Lincoln to Watertown in the muggy May dark
Tickles your throat until you cough

Your mother, aunt, and grandmother go
From being scared of coyotes and the ocean
To hysterical laughter about grandma's English

As the infrequent oncoming headlights scan over you
There is something in that car
Both familiar and awful—you think you see it
Watching you from the woods as you pass
And it will be at home when you get there

Their past—a fever

XIII

Witness: Yes, I saw him beating a stack of illuminated manuscripts
        with the branch from an apricot tree, cussing

Judge: In the middle of Watertown?

Witness: Well I'm no expert, but maybe it's in that middle where the aimless
        lightning hits and sparks the battle of pasts and tongues

Judge: Yes or no?

Witness: Yes

Judge: And what were you doing?

Witness: I had nowhere to go—I was standing near the Charles asking God's help

Judge: Did he notice you?

Witness: God?

Judge: The defendant

Witness: I think so, because he starting speaking some language, aiming at the sky

Judge: Aiming?

Witness: His mouth, I mean

Judge: What came out?

Witness: His insides I guess

Judge: Did you attempt to stop him or try to help in some way?

Witness: No, I had trouble moving

Judge: Trouble?

Witness: Yes, it's hard to move toward someone suffering from consumption

Judge: He was drunk?

Witness: Consumed by some kind of truth beyond truth

Judge: So the answer is yes

Witness: The answer is always yes from now on

XIV

I am making a mask to put over my face
               Slow, deliberate
                                   Like dreamscape erosion
I am constructing it on the dining room table

It is not for hiding or becoming someone else
                    (I've tried both and failed)

                  But the red clay inside the body is calling
For a cover, a shell
        (*Remember how the turtle has the right idea*)

So I am using bits of glass from dad's watch
Old Armenian newspaper clippings from grandpa's notebooks
Grandma's endless rough pen sketches of the same anonymous wide-eyed girl
My uncle's worn black clerical robe, tear-stained and still smoldering
And mom's translucent self-derision—all the throbbing, lord, my inheritances

      (*Don't forget to punch holes for sight and breath*)

XV

Q: Are you expecting a call?

    A: The splintered shield mocks the sweaty palm

Q: Who is lying down on the carpet in Virginia, aged eight?

    A: Late bloomer, your heart is two

Q: Will you straighten your back at least?

    A: There is bravery on the outskirts of the town

Q: Who will testify?

    A:

XVI

Lord, when I speak to you like this, who do I think I am—

Am I not the one usually suspecting you of neglect or even complete abandonment—

Yet all the time I am wrecked by some kind of faith that embarrasses me

Constructs mean nothing to those who break their fists

Upon the waves that keep coming

Soaked through, confessions wash onto your shores, piling up

Ancestors come to gather them, keeping inventory, recognizing their former selves

Some toss the confessions back into the black sea in a moment of fearful déjà vu

We will be them someday and throw back into the dark what was once ours to give

Just the sound of debris hitting the water and disappearing

XVII

Magnifying glass in hand, my grandfather pores over worn atlases, legs
Crossed, feet adorned in thin brown socks

You are here and were there and then there and here you are

I'm a curly-haired boy mesmerized by his intent look
At the yellowish pages, continents and oceans in his lap—
Places where he and his family were in pain in broad daylight

With his long white tailor's fingers he touches the pages, light as dust
His index finger brushes the surfaces of his family's pasts
Until it stops here, this nondescript street in Watertown, Massachusetts

When he looks up and half smiles at me the subtitle reads
Why should this brutish place be any different

At the time, I had no idea

XVIII

Relentless body, you are in the middle of the town
Where you opened your brown eyes in spring

What must have your good smelling dark father
Been thinking in the waiting room, thousands of miles
From the tense dust of Aleppo, and his own father
Who he would never see again

And your ceramic mother, a bloated blossoming cactus
Just wanting you out
       The first and last for her (and you)

They were young, new, and spoke little English
But they could say *I have a son*

They learned it—
There was an assumption of a future

XIX

Born in May when blue sky grows more honest
And rain a moody mistress

                                I keep telling myself

The suns and moons of your name
Offer the kind of comfort that naps for centuries
Right in your driveway

                                Or right in your throat

As you are waking up

                                But I am a fool

Or at the very least melancholy drapery
In the hands of worrying women—

They hold on for dear life to the edges

XX

Stone, toil, tenderness confused by time
That I can only mouth, witness

Ancestors, what is my task—

Everywhere your pasts are deserted
Construction sites, half built, half
Sung, half seen, half born, half
Dead—you ask *How are we to keep*
A straight face—

Large cavities in your lives yawn
From lack of sleep, lack of cover

Nothing makes the animals more frightened
Than the sun's glare upon your wreckage

XXI

Falling over, the part of your story that has been at my throat
Stumbling but not weak
A drunk parent or dull knife

Virginia, you are so humid and look at me funny
From '76 to '83
But I don't blame you

I do the only thing I can think of for a ten-year-old
I pull the covers over my head and pray
The skinny ghosts won't find me here

XXII

The case before you has been dragged
Kicking and screaming through every calm night
Up and down the streets of Watertown, MA and Alexandria, VA
It has bankrupted my compatriots and kin
To the point where they are limp stalks of grain
In the middle of nowhere—they are in my sleep and clothes

See how they are beguiled by their own damage

Clerks and magistrates have marveled at my awkward slurring
That is the only way I can explain how I am still here

Go home the jury finally said (silly jurors)

I have nothing behind me except my futures in my grandmother's softest hair
And my mother's looks that spill over verdict after verdict

So where should I go

Shall I visit the grounds where so many of my family are now in the trees
Shall I dive into Boston harbor but give everything else to Lake Van
Shall I loiter in the parking lots of the Catholic schools where I often waited
Shall I embrace friends that seem to be more and more diluted
Shall I scratch my skin like a lottery ticket

I will give away my winnings as much as I cherish my losses
Shining them like antique silverware

XXIII

Boys and girls, today shall be more stellar than all future suns

Let it be known that birds hopping in small city gardens is genius

Those asleep on buses shall awaken to find their reflections are in tears

We are crippled but shall lie together in the horizon and hum at what comes

We are meandering and lost but shall meet up at the corner and know it as right

If we say *mother* it shall not taste of coal

If we say *father* our loneliness shall not make a scene

The streets shall find themselves covered with our population's grief and ecstasy

Honey shall be in our mouths and when touching skin the rest shall know its place

Those who doubt and squirm in abjection shall drown in their own spittle

Those who do not relinquish petty ammunition or bitter thoughts shall continue blind

Tummy aches shall perish this afternoon

This afternoon we will come out of hiding and the hiding will come out of us

Witnesses everywhere, cup your hands

XXIV

On reel-to-reel tape my mother's voice is someone else's
Calm, collected, warm pools of water, reporting the Iran hostage crisis

When my dad takes me to visit her I have to push a button
To hear her speaking on the other side of the glass

I'm on tiptoes and don't understand what she's talking about
And am barely sure that's her, but it is

Pristine in a way that leaves hunger and nervousness as markers
As though I am a road barely trod, shy in the darkness

At home I press my little face against the shortwave
Radio, looking for her, listening

XXV

Spreading these arms of mine
The bones in my back and neck crack, fine
Plates, sorry hinges, endless branches the tree itself
Does not recognize

                              I listen to the sound

Once, all the nerves were familiar with my body
They lavished me, wrapped me in their fine thread,
Wet circuitry with all sorts of switches and blinking lights
Hidden safe where I could not possibly know myself as a miracle

There are warnings in this life that bind our feet
It becomes impossible to walk upright anymore
Our insides begin to wage war against the outside

Your stories were like that

As high as my branches went your sour tellings went further—
Stumps in every room of that house

XXVI

Whatever this disease, no one put me up to it
No one pushed me toward the door

        On the other side either raccoons or children playing
I can't tell

So I clamor at accountability in your place

I have carved out spaces for you inside me
The soft clay allows it, absorbs the bitter spittle

You even point and designate me *difficult*
And that used to work, it would clench my organs,
Air escaping—a bird falling behind

XXVII

Visiting dad at the plastics factory by the river
The smell signals unchecked commerce and sadness—the din
Eats up the heat and splashes against the concrete floor and walls

All the workers are sweating and doing what they are told—
They make small talk on their breaks, speaking loud over the noise
Because the noise does not give a shit about them

Dad appears from behind some angry machine and walks toward me
With a smile that says *I am sacrificing my life for you and I don't mind*

I do not remember what we used to talk about
But I remember what we talk about now

XXVIII

A violinist loved my mother he would have done anything for her
But that was not what she wanted she wanted to fight it
Fight any possibility of life-on-skin happiness that would be messy
And embarrassing what would people say so she married
My dad when she got to America and she did love him
Eventually I learned to love him she said and I believe her
Because when he slumped over and died at his friends' house
My mother came apart like a bursting bubble like Lego like glass
That's when I knew that she could love something madly in a way
That she did not seem to offer me it startled me seeing
Her on the mauve sofa like that all wet porcelain and cracked
Surrounded by impaired family and a lazy-eyed priest whose breath
Stank with the business of it all just as we all stank in our living room
                                        All together and not

XXIX

Breathless, I am out in the sun undone by all the pulses
Testing me inside, not letting me sleep well

I fight with my address—the lion and gazelle, or two rams having it out

The predator's gaze is the look of exile

On this street then I will finish this line, this lie
It will be a signpost to my brothers and sisters who are wrestling
Themselves silly, unawake and dented by commerce and history

Where are you rushing to—come back and sit here under this sun
See how it grieves in all its light for your haste
It sheds its gold hair for you day after day
Yet you give it only the slightest notice as you propel headfirst
Into having and not having and all the trash in between
Just admit that you are alone and of pure stardust
And be done with it—

There is no hiding place down here

XXX

Somewhere in this world there is a plateau where ghosts rummage
In the soil, stale from being unfinished in life
They cannot see that well as they cruise the empty expanses
But they can smell their blood dried in the dirt, still there

They want to come back into our hearts, their children's children
Who are scattered dandelions barely rooted or not at all

They want to fix the channels that fake the past
Because there were towns and villages, buildings with people in them
There were communities wedded to thousands of years on that land
And the land wedded to them

I'll say nothing about the wind there
Or the confused moon—
They sometimes wonder where everyone went

Millions of ghosts do not count

XXXI

I, Vahan, father of this boy, swear that he will try his best to fly
Not like a falcon, of course, but like a daredevil—he will jump the canyons
Where damaged heritages flood everything in their path

I was not able to reach the other rim—I imagined it
Being closer than it actually is

My failures shall ignite his jets and be ornaments around his wrists

When possible, he must speak his peace and safeguard his insides

                                        This I could not do

His eyelashes shall curve to remind him that nothing is too small
To be stunning and just right, though all around there may be toxins

If there be a god I urge my son to stand up straight, eye to eye
And if there is the likely absence, the same attitude must still apply

He must listen carefully, even to clouds and sounds of construction
For there is a secret whispering light in places we are too arrogant to know

Humor must be available at all times, preferably in his front pocket
For he must learn that at the end of the day it is the only true weapon and shield

And music most of all must blanket his body and calm his blood
Be it sung or spoken, music is the only hint of angels, the only hint

One day when I am gone he must let me be gone and not clench
His teeth onto my dust—

And what cannot be prevented, my son, do not let just wash over you—
If it be Niagara then give it hell no matter what

Tell them your father said so

XXXII

Awake as much as I can be as much as red
      Poppies I have never seen
Congregate by the mountain where mute ancestors clamor
      Not for me or you but for their own faces and breath
Tired of being ghosts in this telling
      Tired of being without punctuation

Mountain, you know who you are, the one at the intersection
Of faiths that charge headfirst against infinity like unbroken horses
Of civilizations that puff their chests while secretly coveting
Of curses tossed between nations and lovers and friends
Myths where the same actors get bored with their sacrifices and visions
The exhale that infects the lungs of centuries

Those bones that will never be found, they belong to my kin

They are buried deep in the guilt of those
Who now live among the gaze of the empty land

XXXIII

O let me slouch in the morning sun as it slouches in me—
America, you will never love me as I love you
And that's that—parting grooms itself and is always ready
        Before we are

What am I to do with this meaty heart—

Birds fly over the closed storefronts as simple as time

Disfigured, I wander the streets picking henbit for you

The rocks in my pockets I keep for myself

XXXIV

And then they waited

Boston was a muddy tired horse in 1966 and it cared not for any particular story
Of tongue-tied families who ended up there on some current of loss or ambition

That kind of water is the kind only the ones in it know
The swimmer or the drowned

But what about the saved
                                         The ones who somehow stay floating even when
They should be at the bottom by now
                                         Their eyes still open

It is so quiet and thick with endings down there—
The weightlessness likes to seduce

But they made it to this place and now wandered the aisles of supermarkets in awe
Not even buying anything sometimes but amazed that they could

Sometimes, in the dark before falling asleep
From where to where, O lord, what is this life

Out their windows in the trees on Hazel Street once in a while
The branches moved in a way that was perhaps god—
They could barely notice anyway, waking in the morning to face the new world again
As though they had never slept in their lives

XXXV

Among buildings and rushing strangers with and without purpose
They begin making their way with mouths slightly open
Each new day lifting and gliding over new regions

What a thing to learn again, like a stumbling foal

Here, this is your new life that you wanted out of necessity, now go and fend
For yourself and see if the dreams and hurt you've been carrying around
From boundary to boundary might finally cancel each other out

Because sometimes it is as simple as math but not as simple—

Calcium deposits, migraines, and clots—these people
Sitting in kitchens, chewing and being chewed

XXXVI

In 1980 my face is getting beaten in
       Because I am not white enough
Two kids drinking 40s start throwing rocks at me, their hands
       Whip my body and face—their violence is clumsy

I see the dirt under their nails—they seem like adults
And like most adults, don't care that I'm a little boy

I take the beating having no clue why I deserve it

They keep saying I'm something—
I keep saying I'm from Boston

XXXVII

So he rubbed his mother's back and thought he might break it
Her skin is white plaster and does not immediately give away her age
But it is worn, and barely holding together her exhausted insides

If she were to break open faded yellow pages from sad books
Would flutter out, the font illegible

XXXVIII

If ever I am straightened and unwound like the most tired elastic
I shall gather in my arms the past—it is nonsense against the skin

If ever I am straightened and let go onto a plush forest path
I shall get lost in the way geese bob on a river at night

And if ever I am straightened and then shot in the back
I shall fall like burnt orange leaves that are most brilliant
                          As they let go of the branch

XXXIX

O let me sleep an unbroken fence around the home our bodies do not fit inside
weighed down weeping sailors we are quarrelsome with our voices and touch our
faces sometimes in disgust at what it feels like I swear to you I am unseamed and
songly just notice the bright air and trembling of your dreams that barely caress
your scalp before turning to sweat and nonsense I see something on the horizon as
they say so why should I too not say it I see something fingers on an aching back or
grass in a sloping field yellowing take me to your bosom and make it all ancient so
that I can take one step forward and listen to the branch creak

the trouble is that loss sits patiently and gleans what it can from us only to use it
later when we spin our tires alone just the noise of friction and mud how did I let
this happen again who keeps pointing a finger at me and walking away like a drunk
former captain who has waived his go at the horizon grandfather I would take your
hand now and slowly lead you I don't know where the parking lot at the mall is vast
and pointless but you tread it with class and even try to joke in broken English with
the Spanish workers at the coffee shop understanding is for the timid and arrogant

two-hearted boy you are a late bloomer shirtsleeves worn and stained with your
secret the girls you've loved are so far away now even beyond nostalgia the
boundaries are disturbing because they are crossed so easily heart pieces
everywhere I don't recognize my own severed selves anymore and what of it on
river banks the hungry squat and touch the brown water and know that they are
unloved and as anonymous as the mud they taste in the water sometimes it is all
there is from day to day and the sun in its hard place

what am I doing here a beating to myself that singes that brings out the salt and
blood from the marrow sounds I can barely utter or make sense of something
about complete loss a cardboard box on a Sunday afternoon when the parents are
away you crawl in and listen

sins failures hands busted from reaching lord shall I toss myself into the coldest
waves or the thinnest air blessed is an ending that wraps you up like a gift let me
hear some Appalachian sorrow in the fiddle be slow and rocking about the way you
touch the strings and push along everywhere in the world mountain tops are the
only manner of knowing anything at all

nor will I know rest and completion just waking up in your clear eyes tells me that I have no way of unloving though I wish I could rescind such foolishness as has been wished for thousands of years with no luck

XL

Tonight there is a path under your feet
The owl shimmers and asks nothing of you
Somewhere a ship makes noise against dark water
Your parents have a memory you cannot begin to know
      See your moonlit hands

Tired of suspecting, tired of being suspect
You clamor like a rabid groupie to have a moment
Where someone else allows
Just allows you
      To be a mess on this earth

Grandmothers everywhere, the children falling
Asleep in your arms under your bad breath
Will eventually want nothing more
Than to become that breath
      When they are all grown and choking

We cannot connect the dots or the bones
We cannot make it better with a kiss or sweater
The lemon is the suck of language in our cheeks
A paper cut on your tongue
      That you keep tasting as you walk

XLI

One day you will arrive at the door
Crusted pale with mud, dry, noiseless
The cough in your heart will tangle itself
Like the fingers of your father at his wake
Tangled the way cells build us, then go

Once, you were unable to sleep alone
But once asleep you were alone as a vase
On a high oak shelf in your grandparents' apartment
Where one is a ghost now
And the other carries around too much in her purse
   She who is often ignored and knows it
   She who is still an orphan-girl on a riverbank
So far from pale you

Oh, how shall we explain it—
There is an elegant difficulty in breath
Just as a heavy airplane flying makes little sense
Or just as the silverback at the zoo gazes and gazes
We are falling so fast it feels still as sandstone

But please, tell me a story anyway
Tell me about the color green and much kissing
Sing me an aria and don't mind the language
It will mind you soon enough

Now, come in

XLII

When you wake each morning you are waking up on earth
You are waking up on rubble, relativity, rhetoric

Pulling the drapes open there it all is, your neighborhood—
Construction, messy dreams, bickering, awkward sex, pets

What do you mean when you shower—there is your body
Naked—you touch it the same way and are often disappointed

Last night there was a dream unraveling in your head like a gift
It offered itself the way a street thinks of you just as you turn onto it

There were people gathered around a dining room table all
Speaking over each other, almost Pentecostal

Pausing to look at you they dropped to a whisper
You wanted to have a seat, join them, be joined

This is what you can remember standing under the hot water
Some of it gets into your mouth and you don't mind

You think *water is in my mouth just as I am in the water*
Nothing dissolves when you think like that

XLIII

There is a body, its breath might as well be a puff of gold dust
Just as your body might as well be an ancient bronze cup

This morning the horizon gathers above tenements, hungry
Or is it just the rush within your chest, a piece of curtain

In your hand, an involuntary thing you do, standing there
On the red carpet, half naked, half everything, your self somewhere

Outside the window in which you barely see a reflection—
It is like a story an immigrant mother might tell

In the July dark, the heat settling in for the night, and a child
Senseless to the wreckage everywhere in the rooms of that house

He plays with the mother's hair, such small fingers lost in heavy curls
The mother gets to the part about the king giving amnesty to the poor peasant boy

She gets to the part where this world and the world all around that boy
Begin to unseam, and what is left is you, looking out onto the street

As the day opens its eyes and tries again
To recognize itself while you begin to dress

XLIV

This you cannot simply inherit, this you cannot
Carry like some muddy crest, a battered legion
Dispensing something but keeping warm
        By staying colder than the cold around the birches

You point at maps and say *there we are*
But the maps hardly register
Your address—pain is in the margins, a ghost
        Trying to get back to a terrain real as heart-blood

The killer still stands over you, says *I did not*
Even as the blade scrapes bone, even
As you hear it—denial like cellophane
        Around a face, a memory, gasping

Now, whispers go on behind closed doors, among
The shine of public relations desks so clean—
Spittle gathers along grins, frightening masks—
        They say *this trauma has become an annoying brat*

History, you reek, just as they reeked, my kin—
Arms, legs, a face jutting out of piles on the Anatolian plains
Is it pointless when told, when given syntax—
        If given back, if we go then, will we be less gone—

Oh, resign from the business class that humors you
Resign from the crayon definition of *us vs. them*
Resign from the way one can become the other—
        The sunlit birches lean slightly, telling us

XLV

Once a cotton-skinned boy, sun-faced
Splashed with little songs and blemishes—
In kitchens mothers and fathers practice the most complicated
American love, or widowed, count rooms
With empty hands—parents, mumbly and stuck

In what seems like winter, they talk about money, rattling—
You listen as hurt gathers around the beige table
Without pageantry—1985
And we're broke, middle class, in the middle
Of walking and falling down

The neighborhood too is like a charming cripple
Brave, able to carry many desires in one basket
But shivering on the inside each twilight—
Locked doors, pulled shades, eyelids shut, covers
Drawn over heads ringing with thoughts of coming up short

If you could reach out like the walnut tree, like the past,
If you could run out of your burning home, singing,
If you could embrace your parents, all parents at once
And cry it out together the way they do in the movies,
And laugh about it as the credits roll

XLVI

Mother, it's so late in the North Sea air—your son's body
Is lit by faint city light, slouched against the past, soft-lipped

Look how his leg twitches, wants to get going, reach
The word *family* again, as though such a thing ever was

Migration doesn't allow you to fathom these words
And that has been our ocean spread silver between us

For years we have been fighting language, tidal
Wave after tidal wave punching sounds

From our mouths, leaving no room for a deep breath—
That is what being rootless is—wading up to our necks

Dazed after a flood no one saw coming
Our feet barely touch the earth under the thick water—

All the way from here, I can see you
Someone's mother, soaked, thin as a glass stem

Pummeled by history and unbelonging—
I want to say you shouldn't be afraid

Though the water is endless and loud
Though it scatters us

You shouldn't be afraid
I can see you from here

XLVII

They have never been on a ship before, let alone
Anything called *sea*—1947
And Beirut is, like them, dumb about the dense future
Already attaching itself like a cataract

Just passengers and waves—a little girl's hand
Slipping in and out of her eighteen-year-old mother's

Two hands, the world on that boarding plank
The sound of shuffling feet in some kind of counterpoint
With the echo of water and the dry swallow in throats

Partial moon sheds what it can—father and grandfather
Talk little, feel their ribcages are lit from the inside

Having made this decision and now, stepping off land,
One or both of them sense control spinning away
Like an angel tired of having to watch

The boarding plank bends from the future, arms
Clutching arms clutching whatever they can carry
Voices consumed by the in-between place, a small crevice—
Even in the most tenuous hand-holding there is
Still more warmth than the most glaring sun
                         About to come

Everyone sits where they can as though at mass
And the off-white ship begins to creak like a song
                         No one has heard before

XLVIII

Waking up at sea, waking up both
Dead and alive, infant and aged, a passing
Thought that unfolds as an electric grid
Like the insides of our bodies

The first ones up are the ones who did not sleep—
Fathers wandering the harsh halls, asking god
Questions answered by the weakness
In their shoulders, the scuff marks and dirt
On their only pair of shoes that contain
Their only feet in this life—they pace like animals

Their children are almost fading
In the arms of mothers already faded
Like the photographs someone might hold years from now

Their small, hot heads merge with the bodies
Of the ones holding them, nuzzled without knowing,
Their radiant sleep unconcerned with the hanging world
About to suck awake their little lives

XLIX

Lord, these mistakes of mine, a wall that leans,
An arm that curls around my neck like a friend's
In a photograph, awkward, not quite posed

What can I do—tell me, and I shall gather
Myself like a bunch of wild flowers
And present it to you, unkempt, unsung

Off-white, like star shards, random
Sparks in a dark home where a family
Pretends everything and everything pretends them

If I could step forward, I would do so
The gut I put my hands on for some comfort
Is not the stuff of legend, just flesh

I roll up my sleeves; how I listen
As this world handles the air by spinning
In the only circle it has ever known

L

Then one day all the lights turned on they came
At the one who was lost came like the eyes of wolves

Standing there as in a fable thoughts were made
From construction paper and the one who was

Lost heard the paper being cut by the hands
Of children who were being cut

By the hands of the future our disheveled teacher
This kind of thing happens

Old men and women asleep know all about it
As do their shy pets and their quiet silverware

The one who was lost had survived being
Lost for that is all that can be done

Caught in that electric white light cousin
To suns moons nervous wrecks among us

What is there an alibi two dangling
Hands at one's side and half-sight

Digging at your chest is useless
There is nothing there that is not out here

LI

In the early dark, birds making
      Their way over us, prayers
            As flesh in air, warm and not forever

Friends, oh my friends, I am guilty

LII

Friend, I want to put my arm around you and say
Something hushed, like a city skyline: your twenties
Were a fake gold chain around your tanned neck
A boxer who keeps losing in the last round

Do you remember all the fog crowded in your head like cotton—
Geography had nothing to offer but distance
And distance had even less

We are wherever we are and can know ourselves only
As a leaf knows its truth; changing, letting
Go, turning into everything else, turning
Into this spot on your shoulder
Where my arm rests now—

I am telling you this because no one told me—
I was a splintered boy, instantly
Fatherless, a decade signed away as though suckered
By a salesman who grins and grins

Thus my twenty-year-old heart was suddenly
Frozen and unable to think straight
I would take it out and throw it at every wall to see
If it would crack and yield anything, maybe shiny
Orange candy or small buttons—
Too often there was just the sound of ice hitting stone

There are those who say that life is about numbers
They say that what is important is not the stars but the space
Between them, the measure from light to dark—
They say equations carry the answers to lonely us

Oh, friend, is this true—convert me then
Turn me into a criminal who sees what there is to steal
Instead of what there is to lose—
I'm ready now

LIII

Perhaps just like this you tilt
> Your head at the station where there's been
>> A goodbye but instead of you or me it

Is the tilt of the Anatolian plains or American suburbs a voice
> Like a thread at the end of a hall
>> A dangling artery

Shyer than all the past's affidavits
> That gather at our feet like newspaper inserts
>> Tossed without a read

LIV

She said it would happen in mid-air
It would confound the atmosphere that's not
Even blue except to us

Hands, our own hands, would make faith
Just as they make us come
Or go, but hardly stay

It was a leap she had in mind, velocity
In the vital organs, prehistoric love
That can only be because it is gone

So I rushed out into the street
I praised schoolchildren as their only father
Spoke fast and hotly to shopkeepers

Placed adverts declaring hope
And never once took my eyes off the ground
Coming at me symphonic and familial

LV

A story, a river, a naked foot –
Once, you knew the weight of these

You knew the spot in the photograph
Where everything present could not be contained

Like a warm arm question-marked under a body
Waiting for a movement, being okay without one

Let the blue-black cold outside be the shield, the skin
Elegant around hot bone, the hot bone before the coming dust

LVI

You sit in the train—dark
The night goes on without
You—what is there
To say—your breath stinks

Migrating particles take their place
They pronounce in you everything
That should and should not be—
Your mother had warned you

Once, all the light was home
In the guts of you, the deepest guts
Of you—and the fear of it
Was like salt in your mouth

Often have you been a reflection
In glass, never etched, never held
Within the silicon as perhaps
Anyone would want to be held

Especially when the light hits like that

LVII

Wet dark wings your caress is time careening
Over every valley and cityscape there are so many

Each barely lit no matter what direction
This is the flight I am the flight and you are stained

Glass depicting whisper after whisper a branch
In rain cold without a person walking by at least

If I say *god* the neck strains as a horse must
As a father must to know what has been missed

It is not impossible that we will be one energy
That is what many hope for while washing their faces

LVIII

The family looks at the river in another new city

       The river bends away and hugs mud whispers in frost

The cold is a testament is the gospel of them standing there

       The feet under them are tired want more dream-song

The melody stutters from geography becomes oak

       The documents in their pockets are barely true anymore

The truth is the braid of the youngest daughter's hair

       The 1960s snap them upon the shore a stick-figure family

The finches in the trees are the only things that move

LIX

Comes a time when all it takes is all missing
From the frame from the lens itself
There's no mechanism for it anymore

If you were to bend backwards to really look
Into the past the way the past looks into you
The river would not be so stubborn

How many times has spring gathered itself
In our towns and hearts making us believe
That somehow things will be different

Let me tell you this: a granular surface
Against your palm is the loveliest way home
Like the pages in the middle of a book or a stone

Once there was the person you were face
Against the glass the road ribboning by
While your father drove your mother sang

Your brown eyes become wet from the sun
That you were told not to stare at
Saturated with light and what we are to become

LX

It is March now dad it is the sweet cold light
Around the trees their bodies stand still for it
Are grateful I think

I too feel that I am inside rough bark
Or that this country is an equation

Meek boy I approach the blackboard to begin it

The faces of people in shops and buses are pixilated
In a way that ignores any ocean or the air in their pockets
Chatter and gestures of hands
One glance that might stick

I wonder about your bones but they do not
Permit me as though to say *mind your reach*
Still I wait in my sleep for clues and instructions
Forgetting them with each new sun my feet
On the cool bathroom floor the water running

You would make a joke about this
You would light a cigarette and make a joke

I believe you

LXI

How are roads made is it like a hand in the damp
Light of winter drawing a line on a map
For a thing to be built when the snow is gone

There must have been a time before you woke up
And realized who you were blinking at the pale ceiling
How quiet was it

Once I too was just part of someone else's hair

I was the dent on the pillow

LXII

Some call it the past an ember
There it is a hot song on your palm
No matter how you look at it it looks
Away

I should not have left
What choice did I have what
Other steps could I take all the lights were on
In the house but not in my father's body

So I walked in took the stairs was led
To a family melting on mauve furniture
Looking at me like the last inch of the last
Strand of light on a winter day yes I remember

My mother's eyes two lanterns way out in a field
How soft black the soil was our mouths became
Full of it so we gagged so we had only
These eyes of ours what could we do

This is the sound of denying whatever forgiveness
Owed me I'd rather you have it I'd rather you
Unclench finally see your hands they are warm they are
The miracle of holding anything at all

LXIII

In this century then hands upon the infrastructure
All the shadows at meetings in thick-glassed buildings
That hum their feet impatient under the table
Where no one can see no wonder we are
Always sleepy and lost
For words

This time no screaming mud or if need be this time
No marching with metal that makes holes
Where there should be none ask yourself
What is the answer to the moonlight hanging
In the moist trees they are never
As naked as we are

You were a child too a basket of shells
And why not we are oceans anyway lapping
Against each other's shores wearing
Everything down that is why we look
To language like a crush who steals glances
At the one who has no idea goes on having
No idea so we have to name what happens
To these achey spaces the way children stretch their arms
When they want to be held or fly away

LXIV

If I tell myself to be a man I should hand out
The speckles of glass that jut out from my skin
It means you had no idea from the start you had
No sense of who lay next to you in the night's static
                                        Listening

So okay I am an insect or a tapping foot fuck the ways
Of this system that drools at binding us like animals
That drools over our dreams while we sleep that mimics
Our measly hearts as we try to reclaim what remains
                                        Outside us

The sinner is the one who harbors rumors and wants
Who keeps shooting arrows at shadows collecting the lint
Of words and days and skid marks throwing fists inside
A vat of gel until the only thing to do is just be still lean
                                        Into the dark shine

LXV

Creaking earth like something coming to me
In my sleep something not symbolic
Because it has a taste a sound
Like a voice saying *it is unwise to reside at the end*
Of a story

LXVI

Until what this is sliced into what I have been until
I came out of the woods of your house the ponds
Of your stank pasts licked at my ankles singing

What was lost fell out of my kid-hands year after year
Half submerged and all the kingdoms let it remain so
I pled for whatever sunlit talk or hint of dry earth

Only your sorry mouths were dry and aimed like crossbows
At whatever flickered in the reeds it was my body there too
Still punctured this is how I woke up